W9-ACB-154

WITHDRAWN

WALDMAN ON THEATER

WALDMAN ON THEATER

PHOTOGRAPHS AND TEXT BY MAX WALDMAN

WITH AN INTRODUCTION BY CLIVE BARNES

AND A PREFACE BY PETER BUNNELL

GARDEN CITY, NEW YORK
DOUBLEDAY & COMPANY, INC.
1971

SALEM COLLEGE LIBRARY
WINSTON-SALEM, N. C.

PN
2111
W3

Grateful acknowledgment is made to the following sources for permission
to use some of the photographs that appear in this volume: Four photographs of Zero Mostel from Zero by Mostel, copyright © 1965 by
Horizon Press, reprinted by permission. Many of the photographs of
the birth and death sequences from Dionysus in 69 have been published
in Dionysus in 69, Farrar, Straus & Giroux, reprinted by permission.
Photographs of The Constant Prince first appeared in The Drama Review, T46, Winter 1970.

Photographs and text copyright © 1965, 1966, 1967, 1968, 1969, 1970,
1971 by Max Waldman.
Introduction copyright © 1971 by Clive Barnes.
Preface copyright © 1971 by Doubleday & Company, Inc.

Library of Congress Catalog Card Number 72-160892
All Rights Reserved
Printed in the United States of America

To the members of the Royal Shakespeare Company's
Marat/Sade—and their New York company manager, Hal Rogers.

93882

The photographer wishes to acknowledge and thank all the participating performers within these pages. All gave freely of their time, talent, and energy. Without their dedicated co-operation to an artistic enterprise, these results would never have seen the light of day—and something very beautiful would have been lost. Thanks are also due to Deborah Kerner for her care and patience in helping put these pages together.

M.W.

"If I forget thee, O, Jerusalem..."

PREFACE

BY PETER C. BUNNELL

MAX WALDMAN is a photographer of exceptional talent and skill. What is more, and this is something of a rarity in photography, he is also a perfect example of that marvelous creature, the contemporary urbane artist. His work has been enthusiastically received in exhibitions at the Museum of Modern Art in New York, at Brandeis University, the La Jolla Museum of Art, and in publications such as *The Drama Review* and *Life*. Working alone with his subjects — not in the theater proper but in his studio — and fundamentally out of his own creative needs, he affirms once again that the acuity of man, not of the camera, is essential for expression in the photographic medium.

There are those who characterize photography as the description of the world in an image, where the image is a kind of replica or object in its own right. The theater, as a sensory experience, is also an illusory image, but it is a transitory one. In this context the photographer seemingly has two choices when determining his photographic approach to a theatrical production. He can produce a picture mirroring and imitating exterior reality, which in this case would

11

SALEM COLLEGE LIBRARY
WINSTON-SALEM, N. C.

be the stage. A second choice is to emphasize the picture itself, that is, to make of the picture an object so distinct that it serves as an extension of the eye — an extension of what is felt about something rather than what is seen. This approach seeks to make the medium visible, whereas the former seeks to make it invisible. It is certainly easier to function within the former, more obviously documentary approach, as most photographers of the theater do, and much more difficult to work in the latter, more inner-directed way. Waldman is clearly interested in this latter direction.

The basis for Waldman's sensuous, evocative, and darkly veiled images is not any bizarre principle of technical trickery. The pictures are straightforward photographs based on the inherent photographic properties of the medium which are the artist's to manipulate and control. What, after all, is a photograph supposed to look like? A description that rests solely on the principles of sharp focus, crystalline detail, and continuous tone is a definition conceived simply out of prejudice or ignorance. Waldman understands this, and his confidence in the medium enables him to utilize it for his personal expressive values without compromise to anyone.

Waldman's approach to a play is what he describes as "restructuring the shapes." Essentially this means that he reconceives the original production for the camera, taking advantage of all those qualities of the freely moving, image-forming optical device. He directs the actors out of their former stage presence and into another existence, and while doing this he reilluminates and again defines the action, thus replacing the original director. The fundamental meaning of the work is not altered, but the visual and non-auditory translation of it is made new. Peter Brook, who staged and directed the New York production of *Marat/Sade*, the photographs of which formed the first significant body of Waldman's work, said of these photographs that they were not the vision of Peter Weiss, the playwright, or himself,

12

but of their work as "seen" by Waldman. This is where Waldman's civility and intelligence come into play. He is intimately familiar with theater, its history and aspirations; with the pictorial artistry of the painters Goya, Rembrandt, and Bosch; and, most significantly, with the modes of human expression that can be viably transmitted through photography.

One cannot do everything in a pictorial image. Waldman has recognized that the classical element of summation in the pictorial arts, whether it be heroics or melodrama, is only extraordinary in individual photographs. He works with the intimacy of the camera, which has as one of its unique attributes the ability to retain ineffable moments from the flux of experience, and through a multifaceted documentation Waldman achieves a grandeur and totality of scope which is a distinctly modern form of photographic summation. In a similar way his pictures may be seen as an advanced form of the radical theater.

In one sense photography of the theater is as old as photography itself, particularly if one views as a kind of drama the posed portraiture of Hill and Adamson done in the 1840s or the anecdotal pictures by Bayard or Robinson, done shortly afterwards. However, the list of truly accomplished photographers who are able to interpret the essence and gesture of the actual theater, as opposed to personalities of the stage, is relatively small. In the latter instance the photographs by Nadar in the last century, and Steichen, Avedon, and Beaton in more recent years, come immediately to mind. But in the former category the work of the late George Platt Lynes and that of Waldman are about the only ones that remain impressed in my own visual consciousness. It is too soon to render a definitive judgment of Max Waldman's photographs, but for now it is clear that as a compassionate artist, interpreting the most vital theater of our day, he is outstanding.

INTRODUCTION

BY CLIVE BARNES

A PHOTOGRAPH is the interpretation of a moment in time. For that split-split-shutter second the scene stops and faces the camera. The shutter descends, as amiably impartial as a guillotine. The instant is petrified, caught irrevocably in an image, capable of enlargement, subject to distortion, and mildly prone to technological rape — which is rape of the nastiest kind.

A photograph is a transaction. There is the man wielding the camera, and there is the object of his lens. Between the two passes the image, and the image — even if it is a snapshot, which it usually proves to be — is, on the most stringent terms, art. A man and his camera focused on a Swiss alp, a Swiss chapel, or a Swiss cow are left very much on their own.

In such simple circumstances the photographer makes his own terms. Presumably he knows the technical rules, and now he is faced with the interpretation of what he wants to say. And alps, chapels, and cows do not talk back. The photographer as artist either snaps his snap — to be shown in some interminable recount of the deathly boring vacation that is destined to become a byword of horror among his dinner-party acquaintanceship — or tries to impose his personality upon the subject. In the latter case the artist becomes a conscious artist; the object is both his canvas and subject, his camera is his brush, its shutter speeds and all those other snares and delusions, his technique.

But when the subject of the photograph is a person, the whole process becomes much more complicated. Here the artist is photographing two distinct things. He is photographing what he thinks of the person, but — much more significantly — he is photographing what the person thinks of himself. This is why the photograph, much more than the painted portrait, is totally revealing. No phrase that a photographer can use on his subject is more useless than "Act natural." We all act very unnatural, trying to hide our faults ("You ought to see my other profile"), pulling in our bellies, vainly attempting not to squint ("I never have been very photogenic"), trying with all our vainglorious vanity at least, the very least, to look interesting. So we collaborate — in either our glorification or destruction. We go to our portrait fate with the very smile we wish to project on posterity. The photographer notes the smile, and with a grim grimace records it on his own terms.

Max Waldman is a great, rather eccentric photographer. He is one of the very few great photographers I have ever encountered, although I have met many undeservedly better known. There is a special quality to Waldman's work. Everything has to be done on his terms. You have here a selection of his theater photographs. Now these are far from being literal theater photographs. To a large extent they are Waldman's criticism and interpretation of the theater. Waldman — and I think I am right here — does not use his camera to record but to comment. Personally I don't think he gives a damn how Charlie Brown plays Hamlet. He is a somewhat arrogant man, and I suspect that *his* main interest is in how *he* sees Charlie Brown playing Hamlet. I like this approach.

16

I can no more see the photographer as a simple recorder of the theater than I can see the drama critic as a simple — or perhaps none too simple — reporter. The first time I saw Max's pictures, a collection of photographs of our mutual friend Marcel Marceau, I knew we had a lot in common in our critical method. I also knew that Max was a critic.

The first theatrical photograph of importance that I know — there are others less interesting — dates from 1867 and is of Ellen Terry at the age of twenty by Julia M. Cameron. In a moment of reflection, fondling a locket, or perhaps crucifix, around her neck, Miss Terry, with her head resting against a background of fleur-de-lys wallpaper, looks the perfect image of her generation. The picture reveals Miss Terry in a way that no piece of writing ever could. And one of the main reasons for this is very simple: Julia Cameron's camera was catching precisely the picture of herself that the twenty-year-old actress wished to portray to the world. Miss Cameron was looking at Miss Terry, but Miss Terry was looking at a camera lens, and among the three of them, a document was produced.

The theater is a fugitive art. Here today, on twofors tomorrow, and gone the day after. What can be preserved? The text, obviously. Often printed and always preserved, the precious words of the playwrights always find a place in posterity. It would probably be just about practicable to gather the texts of most — say three-quarters — of the plays given in New York in this century (Heaven forbid that any one should want to) . Yet these would give us little idea how these plays were played.

In some instances you can get production photographs— scenes of the sets, and the leading actors frozenly posed in some Alaska of non-expression, each face bearing the scar of a self-conscious smile or scowl, each grouping bearing witness to concern or anguish, or else comedians caught, openmouthed, in frigid hilarity. No, production photographs are less than great helps — even though the leading man never squints in them, and the leading lady looks like seven-eighths of a million.

You might think that reviews — especially a selection of them — might give this special flavor. But honestly, no. With the very best critics you always get a decent insight into the play, and often a reasonable description of the way the actors went about their work. The effect is that you can see the play quite clearly, but to visualize the actors is still enormously difficult. Théophile Gautier is regarded as one of the greatest descriptive dance critics of all time. And yet I get a great deal less from his writing on how the Romantic ballerina Marie Taglioni actually danced than I can from the three or four contemporary prints of Taglioni on my walls at home.

These lithographs do not pretend to represent Taglioni; rather they interpret Taglioni. The elusive Taglioni smile, the rather reserved carriage of her arms, the febrile nervousness of her entire dancing are absolutely caught in a few lovingly hand-colored lithographs. These speak volumes — and indeed volumes could not speak so well. This is what I feel about Waldman's work.

Waldman does not precisely record — or if he does, he does not record precisely. For one thing, his photographs of anything are almost instantly recognizable. He likes coarse grains and sudden lights. His pictures are dappled with drama, and he loves those black and white tints of flesh that are photography's particular contribution to the study of the human body. (Personally I have yet to be convinced that color photography is an art form — but then I still have lingering doubts about the validity of talkies.)

If Waldman's style — that bleakly friendly chiaroscuro and those human features like contour maps of inner space — is unmistakable to anyone who thumbs through this book, it must at once be pointed out that this is not a book of photographs in any simple sense. This is not a collection of Waldman's pictures, however agreeable such a collection might be, but quite specifically Waldman's view of the contemporary theater.

Of course I instantly exaggerate. Although as an artist Max goes very deep, as a critic he would hardly pretend to cover even a fraction of the waterfront. This is no comprehensive view of the theater — frankly it is those parts of the theater that have stirred Waldman into action, and also (I imagine, although I have no inside information on this) those parts willing to face the prospect of a Waldman stirred.

First, if you will, look at the portraits of Carnovsky and Mostel. I never had the pleasure of seeing Morris Carnovsky in either *King Lear* or *The Merchant of Venice*, but through these portraits I think I can see it all. The slight overemphasis, the conscious concept of a great tradition, a certain old-fashioned love-it-or-leave-it grand mannerism all combine to give me an assessment, if you like, of Carnovsky in these roles. I know I would have admired him — probably for all of the wrong reasons. But then so does Max.

Mostel I know. To be frank I admire him the happy other side of idolatry as, I suspect, Waldman does. I am familiar with Zero in that darkest of Blooms in *Ulysses in Nighttown* and, of course, as Tevye in *Fiddler on the Roof*. That I shall never be able to forgive Max for not immortalizing him as Pseudolis in A *Funny Thing Happened on the Way to the Forum* is neither here nor there. What he has got of Mostel — the shyly evasive Dublin Jew with a taste for fantasy, and Tevye, the archetypal man with archetypal daughters and pogroms yet — is a brief and perfect candle forever held up to his genius. Show me these pictures of Carnovsky and Mostel in five hundred years' time, and I will be prepared to write reviews of their performances.

When Waldman gets to complete theater productions his sense of interpretation takes a more significant turn.

Looking at most pictures of the theater, you are entitled to feel with a warm glow of confidence that what you are looking at is, at the very least, a frigid and unfeeling document of what actually, at some time or another, took place. Waldman can give you no such comfort. If Waldman wants to photograph a production, he does not go to the theater, cameras in hand, heart in mouth. No, he invites the production along to his studio. And once there, they try to reproduce the spirit of what Waldman thought he saw in the theater.

Waldman's theatrical tastes are here for all to see. He is a Dionysiac, although whether this is by emotional choice or merely because, aesthetically, Dionysus has always made a better photograph than Apollo, I would not know. But he has not photographed Neil Simon and he has photographed Richard Schechner — and everyone buying this book has bought the right to ponder the choices.

The simple thing to say is that Waldman's theatrical predilections are always the most "photographic." This, I suggest, is too superficial. Harold Pinter's *The Homecoming*, stealthily and subtly celebrated here, is not a naturally photogenic play. Yet Waldman, once attracted to it, strikes and captures its specific menace in a quite remarkable, and deftly brief, way. Some of the other plays here are of course photographers' dreams.

Peter Brook's production of Peter Weiss's *Marat/Sade* was, in its way, a theatrical turning point. Not that it was more advanced in its techniques than Brook's earlier *King Lear* — in a sense the reverse was true — but in some special unmistakable way the *Marat/Sade* impinged upon the public consciousness in a fashion that few theater pieces ever do. Look at the pictures Waldman has taken of this and I think you will be able to see why.

The production had a style of its own. Brook himself would be offended by this remark; he is a firm opponent of "style," feeling that the fixed attitude implied by a style is of necessity sterile. But this is not always true, and in *Marat/Sade* the whole production possessed a specially homogenous look. And this look, more than any specific details or individualized portraits, is what Waldman has caught.

At times it might be suspected that Waldman's choices of subject matter are practically fortuitous. Why for example does he give us the Connecticut Shakespeareans in *A Midsummer Night's Dream?* To be frank, this one puzzles me. I can see much more reason in Charles Ludlam's fantasticated *Bluebeard*, less in the APA's forgettably worthy *War and Peace*, and I can understand the bold attractions of the Circle in the Square productions of *Iphigenia in Aulis* and *A Moon for the Misbegotten*. But all these — except for the bright madness of the Ludlam — are conventional theater of greater or lesser conventionality. Max's photographs here are very fine, and yet, personally, I find it is the avant-garde theater where he makes his most positive contribution.

I have already mentioned Brook's *Marat/Sade*. Added to this are Grotowski's *The Constant Prince*, Schechner's *Dionysus in 69*, and excerpts from the life of The Living Theatre, when it was still alive and with us. This is the heart of the book — and it is here that Waldman stands or falls.

Already I have pointed out that these photographs are interpretations rather than simple records, and nowhere is this more true than in the series on The Living Theatre. For example at no performances (at least in New York) did the actors strip naked, but here, inspired by the ambiance of Max's studio, or perhaps merely encouraged by the coziness of his heating system, a lot of them have got down to the buff, and, in this mother-naked condition, surprisingly enough, reach the essence of their performance.

It would be possible to dwell on the individual qualities of the pictures, but they are here for all to see. There are, however, one or two general points that I would like to stress. First there is the texture of the photographs: Waldman uses texture as a signature, as a recognition that the camera is his particular filter to the world. Unlike many photographers, and, indeed, unlike most theatrical photographers, Waldman is not unduly interested in naturalism.

Then I would ask you to look at the movement of the photographs. Most theater photographs are indecently frozen as if intended for use as exhibits in a police court. Waldman has this rare gift as a photographer, an on-going sense of movement. (In passing I must say that I have seen a few of his dance photographs, a field he has not yet extensively explored, and these are most remarkable.) And then — and in most fields of photography I guess that this is what separates the men from the boys — he has an instinctive sense of characterization.

Max is never imposed upon by his subject. The subject offers, he takes, he criticizes, he transmutes. I hope you enjoy these pictures. They are, I think, a document of the theater of our time, and they represent a very personal, silent view. Journalists have a traditional envy of photographers — usually we feel that no one should be so highly regarded for pointing a miracle of modern technology at some event and merely pressing a button. But Max can even restore a journalist's regard for photography — as an art, as a form of criticism, and as a monument to an all-too-easily-forgotten stage.

I forget, although I probably shouldn't, who it was who first called Max Beerbohm the "incomparable Max." I think that in theater photography we have another incomparable Max. Waldman makes the image of the theater live on the insides of our brains. And this is no mean trick.

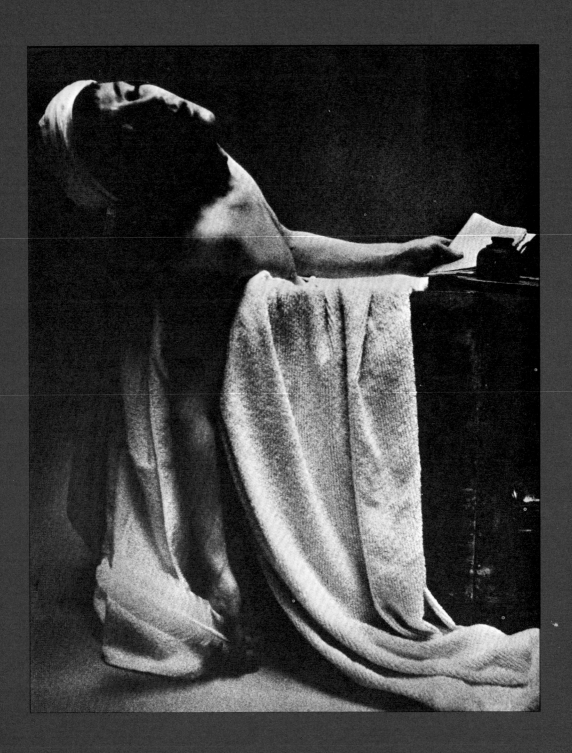

THE PERSECUTION AND ASSASSINATION
OF JEAN-PAUL MARAT
AS PERFORMED BY THE INMATES
OF THE ASYLUM OF CHARENTON
UNDER THE DIRECTION OF THE MARQUIS DE SADE

ABOUT A.D. 1260, according to Joinville's *Chronicle of the Crusade*, King Louis IX established a home for the Carmelite order near Charenton, on the Seine. By the early 1800s Charenton had become a home for the insane, and during Napoleon's regime, the Marquis de Sade was there confined. He had long since fallen from grace as a tribune serving the Revolution. The director encouraged the inmates to put on plays as therapy, drawing audiences from nearby Paris, who came as if attending a circus or sporting event. Several plays written by the Marquis were performed, but none has come down to us. Upon this fascinating background, Peter Weiss fashioned his provocative and polemical play. He leans heavily on Brecht, adapting from him the episodic schema and its herald and singers (narrator and chorus). Weiss is also influenced by Artaud's "Theatre of Cruelty," too much commented upon to go into here.

But foremost, *Marat/Sade* is a philippic, in the best dialectical tradition, against capitalism, money, and property. Despite its political tone, however, the performance presents a strong religiosity. The tableaux format, with its synopsized scenes, is similar to a passion play. Here are elements of ritual death; confrontation of good and evil (or is it one evil versus another?) ; intoned litanies; flagellation, of a delicate perverted sort, when Corday whips de Sade with her unbound hair; and groupings that recall the deposition from the cross.

The abiding genius behind *Marat/Sade's* success was the directorial magic of Peter Brook. It is doubtful whether any other could have brought it to such full realization. His welding together, in a visual sense, the human landscapes of Goya, Bosch, and the elder Breughel; his moving of groups and individuals, each movement with a theme, statement, and development; his perfect balancing of contrapuntal rhythms, not only in spatial relationships but in a verbal progression — all this indicated theater genius at the highest level. Peter Brook, in effect, became the real "star" of *Marat/Sade*.

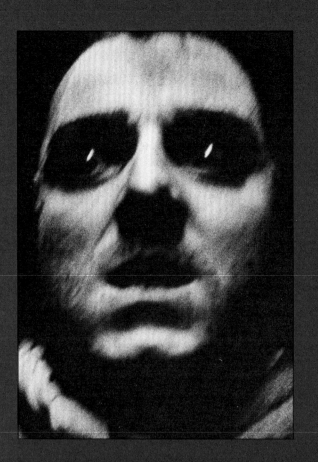

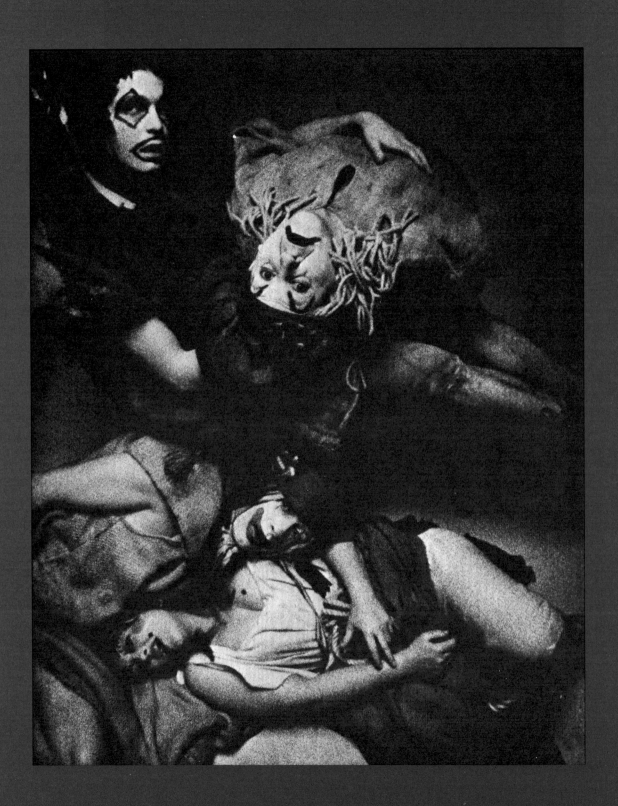

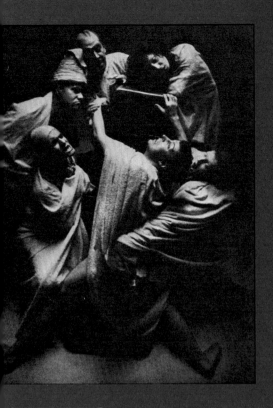

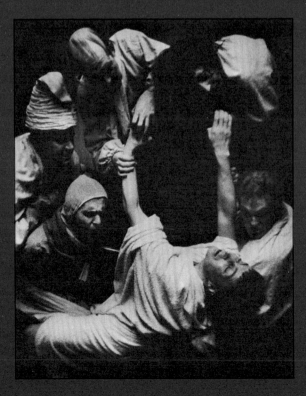

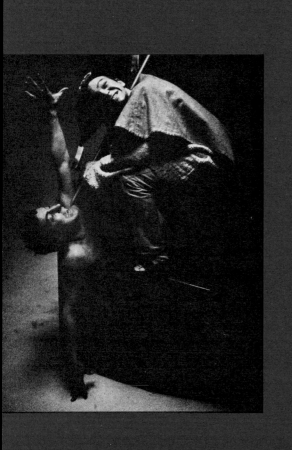
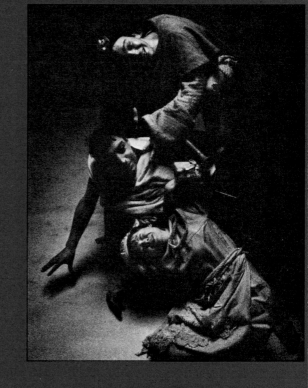

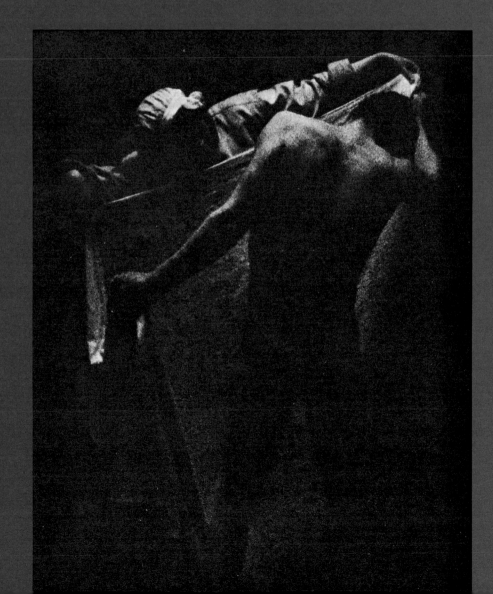

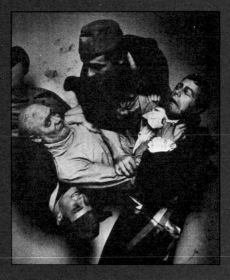
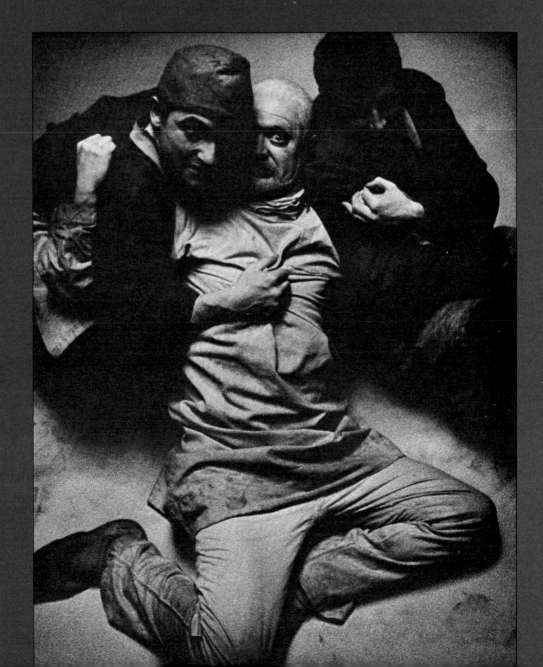

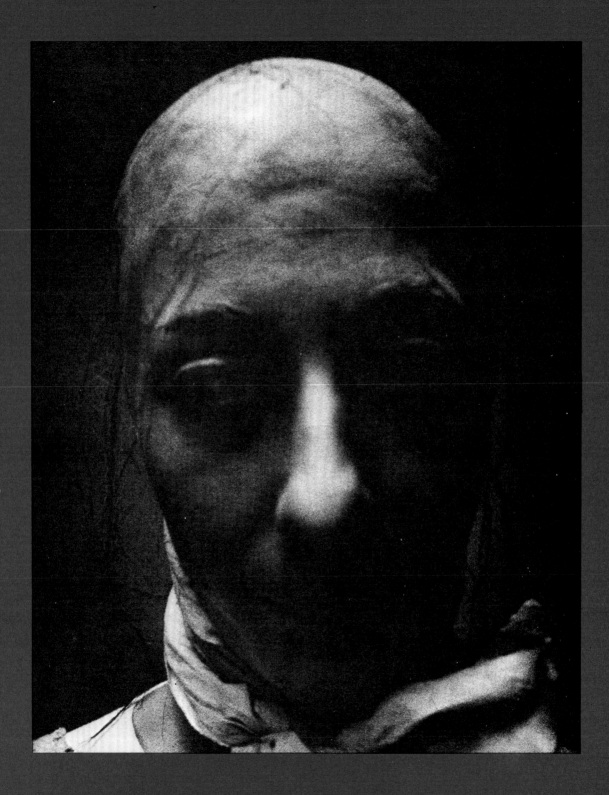

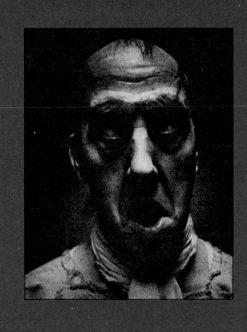

A MOON FOR THE MISBEGOTTEN

THE CIRCLE IN THE SQUARE, in origin, was just that, a theater in the round located on Sheridan Square. Long since removed to a square theater on a straight street, it has become in time the great-grandfather of the off-Broadway movement. The roster of talent spawned by the Circle is most impressive and too extensive to list here.

The most significant success of the Circle has been its raising of the Lazarus corpse of America's leading playwright, Eugene O'Neill. In the period following O'Neill's death, his work quickly became neglected. The Circle productions of *The Iceman Cometh* and *Desire Under the Elms*, directed by Jose Quintero, brought audiences back to O'Neill. *A Moon for the Misbegotten*, which Clive Barnes called "a major minor-masterpiece," received another fine Circle production in this 1968 revival.

MORRIS CARNOVSKY AS KING LEAR

SOME PERFORMERS can etch a personality so indelibly into our memories that long after we have forgotten the details of the production — the other actors, the sets, the words written in criticism — we can remember having been in the presence of greatness and are still touched by it. Such a performance was Morris Carnovsky's *King Lear*.

Carnovsky modeled his *Lear* partly on William Blake's *Book of Job* and *The Last Judgment* of Michelangelo. His performance was classical in every sense of the word: in speech, costume, mood, and posture. Biblical and epochal, they are both timeless commentaries on our frail human condition, and they are echoed in *Lear*, another distant legend reaching far back into the night of tribal myth.

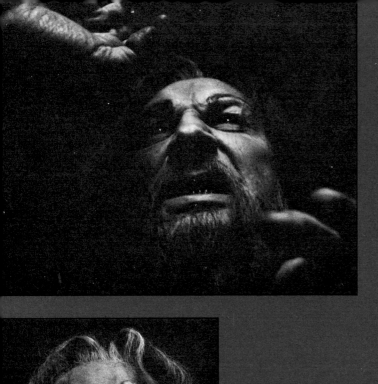

MORRIS CARNOVSKY AS SHYLOCK IN THE MERCHANT OF VENICE

CARNOVSKY's portrayal of Shylock reached the expected peak in rage, arrogance, and bewilderment. This fiery Shylock stood in marked contrast to the rest of the company, which was dominated by actors playing it "cool." Carnovsky's voice was operatic in its range and depth, and in its intensity and controlled tremolo. He played the earlier scenes with unexpected restraint, but unleashed a torrent of emotion with the impassioned speech, "Hath a Jew not eyes." Carnovsky frequently struck the studied pose of the classic Shylock, but when told that Antonio's ships had been lost at sea, he delighted us with a short, wild hasidic dance. It was a memorable moment in the theater.

THE LIVING THEATRE

THE LIVING THEATRE is an encampment of gypsies foraging off the land, an unorganized, scraggly army on the march. Non-violent in theory yet vulnerably explosive, they combine a Rousseau-ean natural goodness with the scatalogical Artaud. A rather loose atmosphere prevails. Clothing and hair styles run the extremes of today's youth. New and fanciful names replace baptized ones. Poverty is their badge, dispute their weapon. Theirs is like the primitive communism practiced by the early Christian sects. Wherever they go they arouse the gamut of responses: adoration from the youth, hostility and open warfare from an outraged, conservative citizenry.

Their theater touches all the contemporary reference points: Brecht, Artaud, and Marx. Themes are thrown together and tested to push their message further, to harass the patience of the smug. If they set people on edge, if they embarrass, irritate, and annoy, this is precisely their intent. The plays move in a time element not unlike those of the Eastern theater, where performances last six hours or more: Kabuki, Kathakali. There are periods when the members of the cast just sit about and stare at the audience or themselves; sometimes they endlessly repeat phrases as in celebration of the mass.

Paradise Now is not so much a play as a blueprint for revolution. All distinctions between stage and orchestra are obliterated, between audience and actors, between those who paid for choice seats and those crowds crashing in literally to usurp and evict the front-row tenants. The stage swarms with these new "decisioners" in this chaotic revival meeting carried on with evangelical fervor. The safest place is in a balcony (if there is one) where one can watch the heated arguments raging in every corner of the auditorium.

The Living Theatre is nothing less than a latter-day Children's Crusade to free the new Jerusalem from the Moloch of capitalism. Each member of the group is not an actor but a proselytizer, seeking to persuade the spectators to drop their restrictive behavior and join them in the unfettered freedom of anarchy. This goes beyond any theater we know, for it is a theater that is life itself and not a prosceniumed substitute.

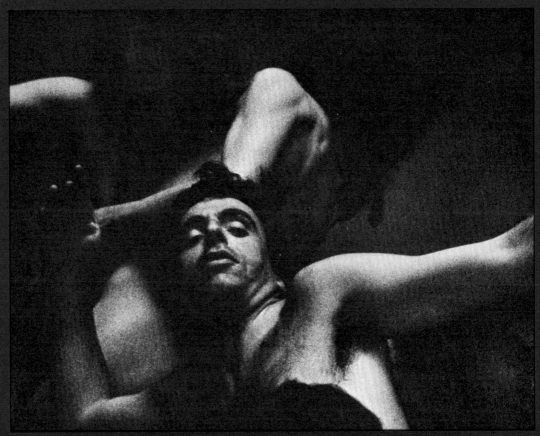

DIONYSUS IN 69

DIRECTED BY Richard Schechner, *Dionysus in 69* was, in his own words, adapted "somewhat after Euripides' *The Bacchae.*" This disarming phrase did not prepare the invitee ("spectator" is somehow wrong) for what was really an assault on traditional theater. Press reactions ran the gamut: "crucifying the classics," "amateurish," "a leap forward," "obscene." But no review could adequately describe the experience of being there.

In this play, if it could rightly be called that, Schechner brilliantly interwove the Euripidean text with the contemporary scene. Much as Homer's *Odyssey* illuminates Joyce's *Ulysses*, so here the clues of the past remind of the present — so much so that one is surprised at how much of Euripides Schechner kept intact.

An environmental wrap-around staging eliminated the typical framing archways. Little remained but the actors, their actions, and their words. No curtain lifted to announce the beginning. Members of the audience, allowed in singly with the actor's preparatory exercises already in progress, found their places on the floor or on tower scaffolds. During the performance the actors moved from their patch stage to mingle with the people, crawl on their bellies under the scaffolds, and leap from tower to platform. The audience, whether climbing down from their perches to join the action, or merely content to observe, became part of the over-all design.

They were witness to the degrading of Pentheus by Dionysus, the revels with everybody dancing to flute and drum, Agave's recognition that her king/son lies dead, and Dionysus' final harangue to the citizens of Thebes foretelling their doom and the city's destruction. The strongest images were "epiphanies": Birth Ritual and Kill. Schechner adapted the Birth from an Asmat tribal rite, remembered from a film on New Guinea. At the end, *Dionysus* stopped abruptly. The actors just cleaned up the "blood" with buckets of water and large brushes, leaving no time for applause.

The matter-of-fact nudity of The Performance Group surprised many. This was the first time so many naked bodies had been presented on a New York stage before a public audience. There was no coyness in the act of disrobing, no dimming of lights. The actors, standing in a square, quietly took off their street clothes, costumes of a sort, and arranged themselves for the Birth Ritual. Done with, they nonchalantly dressed and proceeded with the performance. The same was repeated for the Kill. Since then, many productions have featured nudity, but none has reached the emotional perfection of these epiphanies from *Dionysus in 69.*

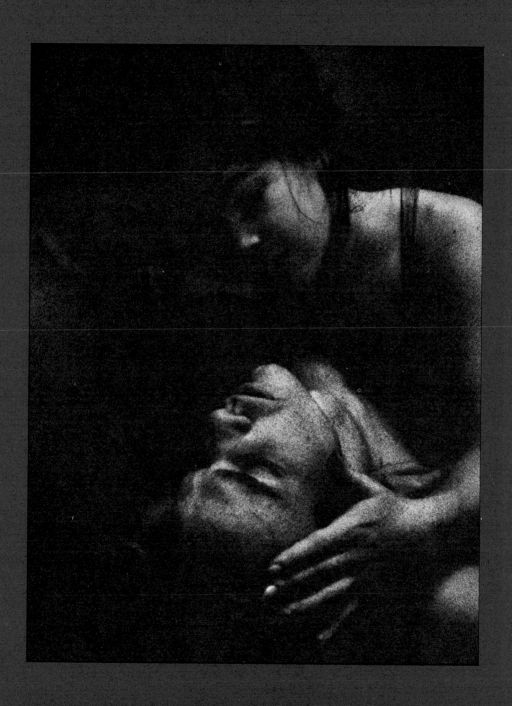

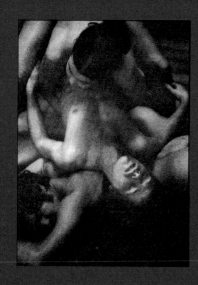

o

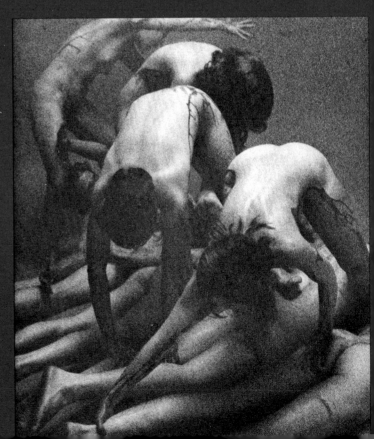

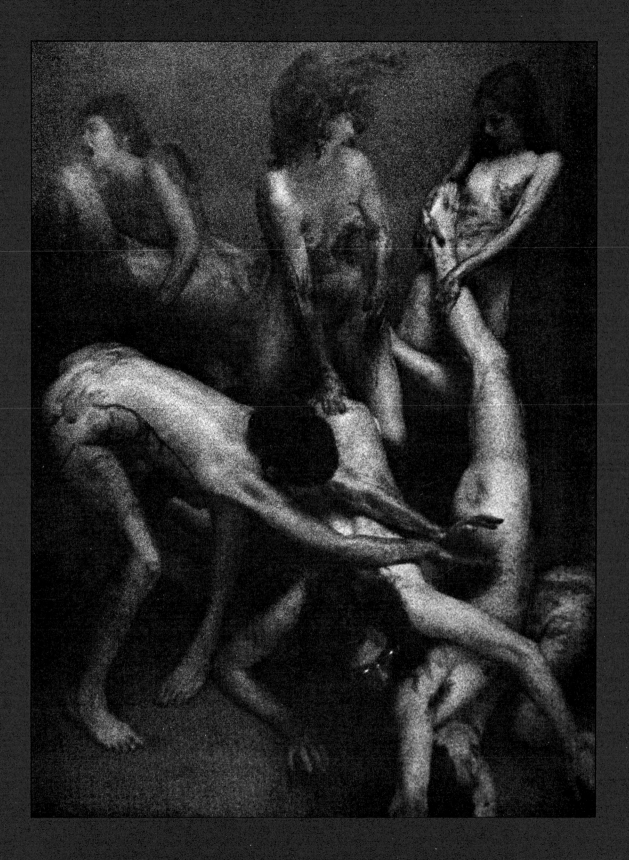

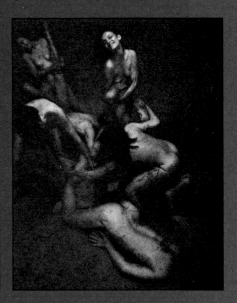

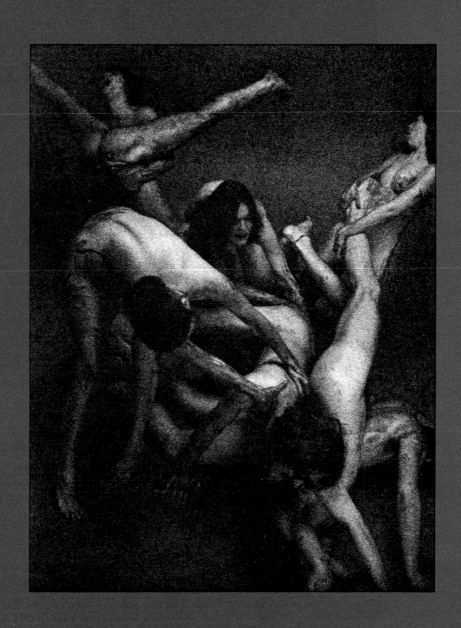

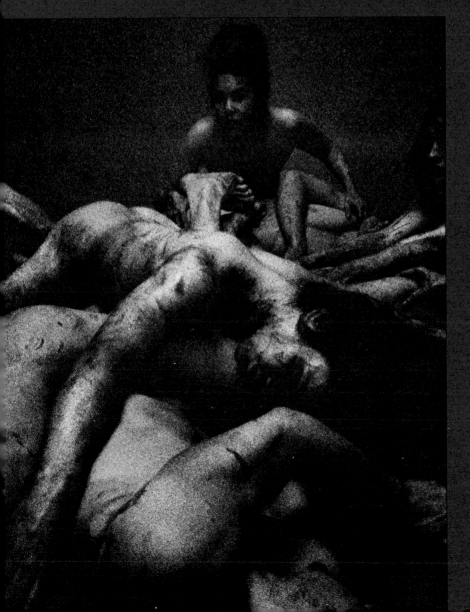

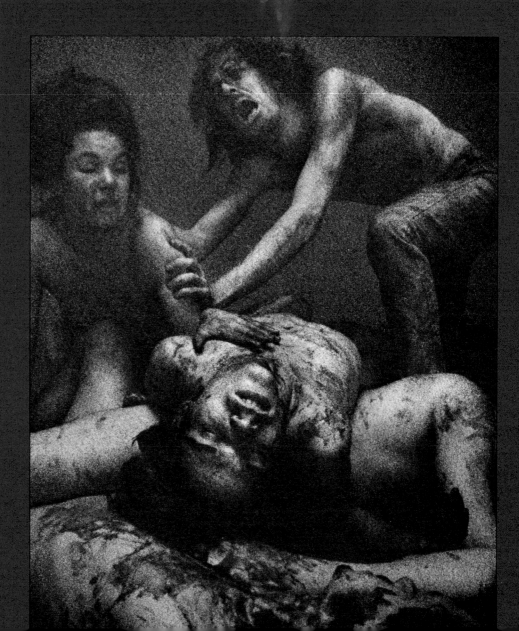

THE HOMECOMING

THOUGH SET on a summer's day, *The Homecoming* is a dark, cold play. The members of this North London family seem to exist both in winter and in night. This is not so much a play as an isolation, in which everything is suspended in a void. Filling the spaces are the rhythms of disassociated sounds: the rattle of a newspaper, the creak of a loose board, a disconnected word that settles in mid-air. It is a drama of silences, of pauses and frequent halts. Pinter conjures up a bleak vacuum, supposedly empty, but upon entering, we find to our discomfort that it is peopled with the likes of us.

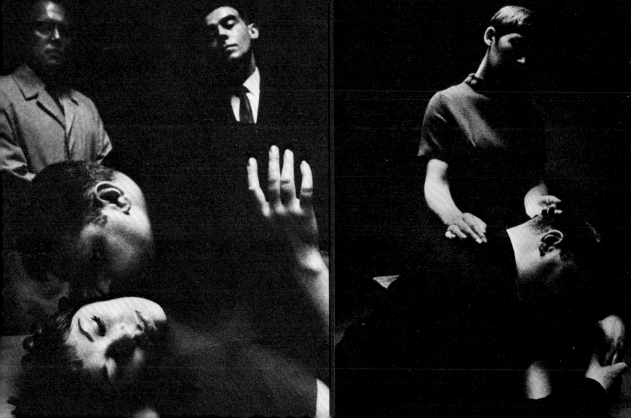

IPHIGENIA IN AULIS

NEGLECTED IN HIS later years by the Athenian citizenry, who had grown weary from endless wars, Euripides' work suffered a long decline and almost total eclipse. Kept alive by the devoted few, his plays now reach across the centuries to touch us with a new relevance. *Iphigenia in Aulis* is not a stylized retelling of the sacrifice of a little girl, but a power struggle between men of strong will, who use the gods to justify their acts. This Circle in the Square production of the play makes us question how far we have come from our primitive yesterdays.

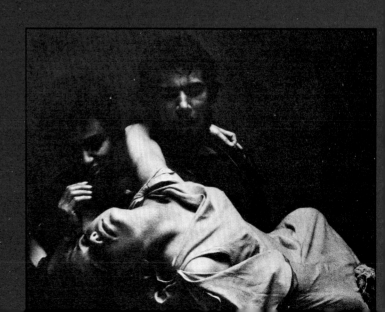

WAR AND PEACE

ERWIN PISCATOR, an archexperimenter with the episodic play form, left his native Germany during the Nazi era to come to the United States. Piscator settled in New York, while his compatriot Bertolt Brecht, who also fled Nazi Germany, made his temporary home in Santa Monica. At war's end each playwright returned to a separated Germany and a divided Berlin, but the influences remaining behind have lasted a generation. Example: Judith Malina Beck studied with Piscator, translated Brecht's version of Euripides' *Antigone*, and presented it by The Living Theatre as an antiwar play. Culture patterns weave fascinating, incestuous paths, crossing national boundaries and time spans.

So it is appropriate that in Piscator's adaptation of Tolstoy's gigantic novel, the object of attack is not Napoleon, but the Janus-headed duumvirate of Hitler and Mussolini. By inference, 1812 becomes our time, our place.

GROTOWSKI

THE COMING of Jerzy Grotowski's Polish Laboratory Theatre to America was awaited with eager anticipation. His credentials were in order: university-trained student of theater, heir to Stanislavski, with specific methods of actor training and stage techniques; intellectual enough to embrace Meyerhold, Artaud, the Kathakali; and strong enough to have influenced Peter Brook, The Living Theatre, The Open Theatre, The LaMaMa Experimental Theater, The Performance Group, Jerome Robbins, The Manhattan Project Company; and farther west, The Minneapolis Firehouse Theatre, The Theatre Company of Los Angeles, and the Theatre Five of San Diego. He had already captured the idolatry of acting students everywhere, along with the influential resident professor/drama critics on university campuses. Above all, Grotowski, with his own company, would provide examples for study and inspiration.

The earmarks of a Grotowski production are by now well known, having been incorporated into avant-garde theater direction. Members of the audience are introduced one or several at a time, the rest waiting their turn. Seating is in every style and description except in traditional rows — upon floors, planks, or platforms arranged in haphazard fashion. Performances start swiftly and end abruptly, rarely lasting more than an hour. The action may take place in and around the spectators, usually limited in number. There are few or no props; the actors wear simple costumes or street dress. The play is episodic, at times with no apparent connecting link. It may be plotless or derived (albeit remotely) from the classics, the Bible, Calderón, Marlowe. Emphasis is on choreography and acrobatic body movement. Speech is suppressed in favor of sound effects: grunts, hisses, body slapping, clapping of hands. The actors make percussion instruments with whatever comes to hand, by knocking on chairs, with wooden pipes or tambourines; creating primitive rhythms that are in turn quiet or menacing, depending upon the mood required. There is little color — even a red cloak may seem drained of its hue.

The most impressive part of the Grotowski experience was Ryszard Cieslak in *The Constant Prince*. He has gone beyond the traditional meaning of the word "actor," belonging more to the legend of Nijinsky. In his animal sounds was the heart-rending anguish of Beethoven's *Grosse Fugue*. In his fleshly movements was the flayed ox of Rembrandt and Soutine which cries life though dead. His was a gaunt Giacometti stripped bare and skeletonized before our eyes.

After each production, one felt something out of place. The church, set on a bustling city street, seemed wrong. The forty, ninety, or one hundred spectators, though few by normal standards, were far too many. The presentations should rather have been given in a small private chapel in some isolated cemetery, where the witnesses, perhaps three or four in number, accidentally wandered in, as if happening upon some mysterious, sacred ritual.

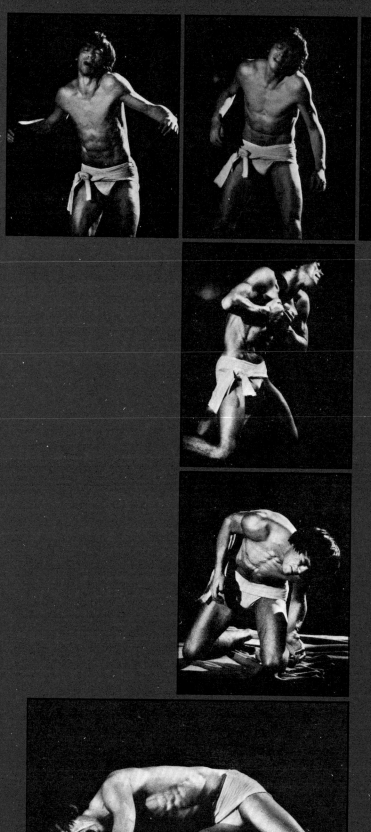

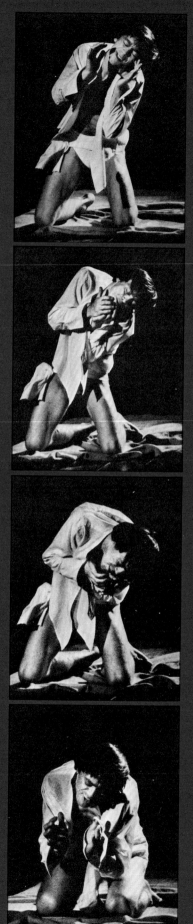

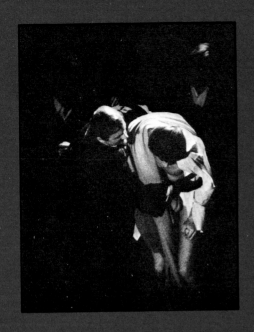

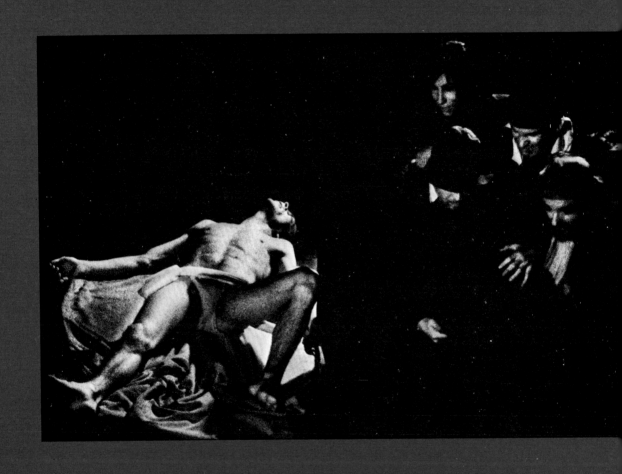

A MIDSUMMER NIGHT'S DREAM

In 1662 Samuel Pepys recorded in his diary that A *Midsummer Night's Dream* was "the most insipid ridiculous play that ever I saw in my life." And every age since has borne him witness with their witless productions. Yet the *Dream* miraculously stays alive in spite of all the plundering and bowdlerism to suit contemporary tastes. The popular appeal of the fairy story of Oberon and Titania, and of the country bumpkins, Pyramus and Thisbe, have made A *Midsummer Night's Dream* one of the most frequently produced of Shakespeare's comedies. This production was directed by Cyril Ritchard for the American Shakespeare Festival in Stratford, Connecticut.

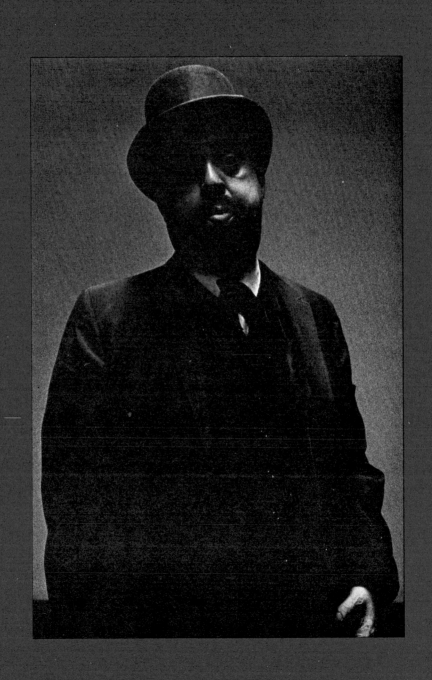

ZERO MOSTEL AS BLOOM
FROM ULYSSES IN NIGHTTOWN

FROM HIS EARLIER overexaggerated antic humor, there was little to presage Zero Mostel's transformation into the archetypal perfect Leopold Bloom. Here was, perhaps, the most brilliant single tour de force of the actor's art to be seen in a lifetime. Mostel not only understood Joyce in every nuance, from remembered fact to favorite fiction, but he became, or rather *was*, Bloom himself.

Mostel is surely one of the great comic geniuses of our generation, though not an actor in the classical sense. He does not speak with that fine declension of trained voice that tingles the back of our necks with its timbre. When he embroiders, he often shades the line from bawdy to vulgar. But in the totality of his art, in his inimitable style, he has no peer. He belongs in that line of great clowns numbering Chaplin, Buster Keaton, Jimmy Savo, and Harry Langdon. In versatility, the only performer he can be compared with today is Marcel Marceau.

Few of us will again see the likes of Mostel as he was in *Ulysses in Nighttown*. This performance, however, marked the turning point back to recognition of Mostel as a serious artist.

ZERO MOSTEL AS "TEVYE" FROM FIDDLER ON THE ROOF

Sholem Aleichem's "Tevye" stories, from which *Fiddler on the Roof* was taken, were written in the days of pre-Hitler innocence. It was, however, an innocence swathed in the barbed wire of ever-present pogroms, the memory of which pervades what is otherwise a bittersweet and often simplistic entertainment.

The word *schtetl* has found its way into mass culture, but theatergoers will understand my definition: a *schtetl* is a body of land surrounded by Zero Mostel, the original Tevye.

BLUEBEARD

ONE HAS TO burrow down many a rabbit hole to come up with the Mad Hatter genuis of a Charles Ludlam. He brings together on a single frame fragments of Picasso; H. G. Wells (*Island of Lost Souls*); pulp science fiction; the high radio humor of the '30's and '40's; Bela Bartok's one-act opera, *Bluebeard's Castle*; plus our gentle monster, Boris Karloff — then unsystematically shatters them all before they have had time to stay around and fraternize. If we look fast enough we can glimpse Shakespeare, Gilbert and Sullivan, Italian commedia dell'arte, the Marx brothers, and Cio-Cio-San. To give this preposterous tale a rather loose pedigree, refer to Antonin Artaud's *The Theatre and Its Double* (Grove Press), Chapter VIII, "The Theatre of Cruelty" (First Manifesto) under "The Program," #4: "The story of *Bluebeard* reconstructed according to the historical records and with a new idea of eroticism and cruelty." That about sums it up. But Ludlam's endless miscegenation is far too complete to sort out the pieces. To call it high art is to mistake the local amateur night for a Grotowski *Sturm und Drang*.

English is a tongue not easily spoken by this Ridiculous Theatrical Company. Words are hissed, spat, purred, and sibilated, but rarely spoken. Language is misshaped, tortured, and used throughout in its purest form — as cliché.

No matter where you sit, they will get you with a half-hearted riposte. There are no travesties too great for them to take up and crush.

To me, *Bluebeard* is the most perfect example of its genre. One can detect an obvious brilliance here, but he must do everything possible to avoid recognizing it. One must also resist all intellectual blandishments or high claims to delicate taste, in favor of wallowing in the low trough of gut-level enjoyment.

Fractured victorianism is rampant, along with mixed spoonerisms, astrology, alchemism, a live snake called Larry, smoke, brimstone, and, of course, a climactic *deus ex machina*. Here the pun is ancestor to the jape. We have everything: violence, sex (but then who doesn't, of one sort or another?), mixed identities, and rompish seductions. Somewhere in all this melange weaves the story of our hero, Bluebeard/Ludlam, the mad scientist trying to create a third genital. Some would say that he has succeeded?

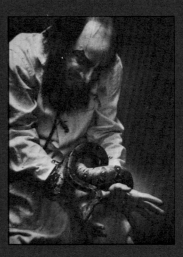

CREDITS

THE PERSECUTION AND ASSASSINATION OF
JEAN-PAUL MARAT AS PERFORMED BY THE INMATES
OF THE ASYLUM OF CHARENTON UNDER THE
DIRECTION OF THE MARQUIS DE SADE.
BY PETER WEISS

Production: Royal Shakespeare Company
Director: Peter Brook
Costumes: Gunilla Palmstierna-Weiss
Clifford Rose, Brenda Kempner, Ruth Baker, Michael Williams, Freddie Jones, Hugh Sullivan, Jonathan Burn, Jeanette Landis, Robert Lloyd, Glenda Jackson, Ian Richardson, Susan Williamson, Patrick Magee, John Steiner, Mark Jones, Morgan Sheppard, James Mellor, Ian Hogg, Henry Woolf, John Hussey, John Harwood, Leon Lissek, Mary Allen, Michael Farnsworth, Maroussia Frank, Tamara Fuerst, Guy Gordon, Sheila Grant, Michael Percival, Lyn Pinkney, Carol Raymont, Heather Canning, Jennifer Tudor, Timothy Hardy, Stanford Trowell, Patrick Gowers, Richard Callinan, Michael Gould, Nicholas Moes, Rainer Schuelin.
Photographed in 1966.

THE LIVING THEATRE

Steven Ben Israel, Mary Mary, Jim Tiroff (Olé), Nona How-
ard, Henry Howard.
Directors: Judith Malina Beck and Julian Beck.
Photographed in 1969.

A MOON FOR THE MISBEGOTTEN

BY EUGENE O'NEILL

Production: Circle in the Square
Director: Theodore Mann
Costumes: Domingo A. Rodriguez
Salome Jens, Mitchell Ryan, W. B. Brydon
Photographed in 1968.

KING LEAR

BY WILLIAM SHAKESPEARE

Production: American Shakespeare Festival, Stratford,
Connecticut
Director: Allen Fletcher
Costumes: Will Steven Armstrong
Morris Carnovsky.
Photographed in 1965.

DIONYSUS IN 69

BY RICHARD SCHECHNER

based on Euripides' *The Bacchae*
Production: The Performance Group
Director: Richard Schechner
Samuel Blazer, Remi Barclay, Jason Bosseau, Richard Dia,
William Finley, Joan MacIntosh, Patrick McDermott,
Margaret Ryan, William Shephard, Ciel Smith.
Photographed in 1969.

THE HOMECOMING

BY HAROLD PINTER

Production: Royal Shakespeare Company
Director: Peter Hall
Costumes: John Bury
Terence Rigby, Lynn Farleigh, Michael Jayston, John
Harkins.
Photographed in 1967.

THE CONSTANT PRINCE

BY CALDERON DE LA BARCA,

ADAPTED BY J. SLOWACKI

Production: The Polish Laboratory Theatre
Director: Jerzy Grotowski
Costumes: Waldemar Krygier
Ryszard Cieslak, Antoni Jaholkowski, Rena Mirecki,
Zygmunt Molik, Zbigniew Cynkutis, Stanislaw Scierski.
Photographed in 1969.

WAR AND PEACE

BY LEO TOLSTOY,

ADAPTED BY ERWIN PISCATOR

Production: APA-Phoenix
Director: Ellis Rabb
Costumes: Nancy Potts
Stefan Gierasch, Alan Fudge, George Addis, Harley
Hackett, Michael Alan MacDonald, James Whittle.
Photographed in 1967.

IPHIGENIA IN AULIS
BY EURIPIDES
Production: Circle in the Square
Director: Michael Cacoyannis
Costumes: Michael Annals
Jane White, Mitchell Ryan, Gretchen Corbett.
Photographed in 1968.

THE MERCHANT OF VENICE
BY WILLIAM SHAKESPEARE
Production: American Shakespeare Festival, Stratford,
Connecticut
Director: Michael Kahn
Costumes: Jose Varona
Morris Carnovsky, Maria Tucci, William Myers.
Photographed in 1967.

A MIDSUMMER NIGHT'S DREAM
BY WILLIAM SHAKESPEARE
Production: American Shakespeare Festival, Stratford,
Connecticut
Director: Cyril Ritchard
Costumes: Robert Fletcher
Diana Davila, John Cunningham, Dorothy Tristan, Jan
LaPrade, Cyril Ritchard, Jane Farnol, Jerry Dodge, Robert
Frink, Tom Lacy, Carl Don, Mylo Quam, Rusty Thacker,
Ian Tucker, Laura Michaels.
Photographed in 1967.

ULYSSES IN NIGHTTOWN,
ADAPTED BY MARJORIE BARKENTIN
FROM JAMES JOYCE's *Ulysses*
Director: Burgess Meredith
Costumes: Herman Rosse
Zero Mostel.
Photographed in 1965.

BLUEBEARD
BY CHARLES LUDLAM
Production: Ridiculous Theatrical Company
Director: Charles Ludlam
Costumes: Mary Brecht
John D. Brockmeyer, Eleven, Mario Montez, Charles
Ludlam, James Morfogen, Sebastian Swann, Lola
Pashalinski, Bill Vehr, Black-Eyed Susan, Lohr Wilson.
Photographd in 1970.

FIDDLER ON THE ROOF
BY STEPHEN SONDHEIM
   based on the "Tevye" stores by Sholem Aleichem
Director: Jerome Robbins
Costumes: Patricia Zipprodt
Zero Mostel.
Photographed in 1965.

MRB—BIC